WILDSONG

Wildsong

Poems and stories of

SHEL O'TOOLE

Shirley O'Toole

Copyright © 2024 by Shirley (Shel) O'Toole

All rights reserved. No part of this book may be reproduced in any manner whatsoever without written permission except in the case of brief quotations embodied in critical articles and reviews.

First Printing, 2024

ISBN: 9-781446-616147 - Paperback
978-0-9756192-1-6 -E-Pub

First Published: February 2024

Published by: Shirley O'Toole
Ballarat East Victoria 3350

Dedicated to the poets and artists, singers and songwriters,
performers and audiences who helped me to know I belong
in the community of artists.
And to mum and dad, who gave me life and encouraged curiosity.

I acknowledge the Wadawurrung people as the traditional owners of the lands that I live and create on. I pay my respects to their elders, past and present.

FOREWORD

This book has been years in the making. An artist friend encouraged me put my work into a book back in 2013. I wasn't ready then because I hadn't yet accepted that I was an artist.

I've always written poetry. It was a very private practice and I seldom shared what I had written. In 1996 I started writing songs. I was comfortable sharing my songs but not my poetry. Until Darwin. I was busking in Smith St Mall in 2013 when I was told about an open mic night at Happy Yess and encouraged to go along, which I did. It was a great place to meet other musicians, poets, theatre makers, artists and arts lovers.

I rocked up one night and it was Spoken Word night and to get free entry I had to perform. At the time I was living on busking and part-time work so free entry meant I could afford an ice-cold beer. I was apprehensive, conflicted. Sharing my poetry seemed like I was exposing my soul. It was hot, I wanted that beer. I performed and I loved it.

In 2014 I won the Darwin Poetry Cup and the Darwin Poetry
Slam, apparently the first woman to do so. I got to represent Darwin in the National Poetry Slam. I was amazed and incredibly proud that I, "a girl from Murrami" got to perform at the Sydney Opera House.

These achievements cemented my place in the arts community and it was Darwin based playwright Mary Anne Butler who challenged me to see myself as an artist.

I think my Celtic heritage is the source of my creativity. I have fond memories from childhood of being dragged out from under tables where I'd fallen asleep while my father played accordion or fiddle at dances and family celebrations. I remember fireplaces, flames, stories and straining to stay awake so as not to miss anything.

Regardless of whence it came, I am blessed to have the gift of creative expression, to **be** an artist.

May you enjoy Wildsong.
Shel

CONTENTS

Dedication	v
Foreword	vii
Myth Magic & Mother Nature	1
1. Wildsong	2
2. When Raven Came Dancing	3
3. Lunacy	4
4. Pantheist	5
5. The Wind	6
6. Dark Moon	7
7. The Shaman	8

Life ... 9

- 8   Death of A Brother ... 10
- 9   Eleven Percent ... 12
- 10   Bah Humbug ... 13

Love and Lust ... 14

- 11   The Growing Need ... 15
- 12   You ... 17
- 13   Sensuous Sunshine ... 18
- 14   Haiku Song ... 19
- 15   Monsoon Moist ... 20
- 16   Green Finger ... 22
- 17   Nonchalant ... 23
- 18   Unravelling ... 24

Politics and Power — 25

- 19 Ode to the Last Story — 26
- 20 Abbott Stew — 28
- 21 Soil-can you dig it? — 29
- 22 Drone — 31
- 23 Suffer not the little children — 32
- 24 Rise of the Angry Woman — 33
- 25 Transmuting Poison — 35

Myth Magic & Mother Nature

| 1 |

Wildsong

In the dreaming her voice sang her into existence, a wild, spirited woman with hair the colour of fire.

When they found her, naked and strong combing her tangled tresses with fingers like claws the people made sacred symbols to protect themselves.

Unable to speak their language, she sang to them and as she sang, fish jumped from the big ocean to land at her feet.
They recognised her then and brought her fruit and honey bags.

In the north, by the Arafura Sea, rumours abound.
After 40,000 years Wildsong has returned in the guise of a mortal.
When she sings the people recognise her
and bring her gifts of currency.

| 2 |

When Raven Came Dancing

A Raven came dancing with A broken wing
Reminding me of Lore

Mabh and Morrigan call time for battle
time for truth telling

When egos are the only victims
yet women and children remain prey
Raven's fly into war

| 3 |

Lunacy

The moon was in its fullness
Tugging at my emotions
Like it draws waves to the shore
Ebb and flow
Raw

The moon was in its fullness
I was the wolf
Howling
Locked up inside
Yeaning to be prowling

The moon was in its fullness
I couldn't see
The malaise that had me in its grip
Was surely lunacy

| 4 |

Pantheist

Grazing the hills and valleys with my footsteps my soul rises up within me

Immersed in the waters of the cool clear lake
I am all the fish that ever swam

In the tallest tree with the wind blowing through the branches
I am the eagle and the kite, the black cockatoo

as butterflies skitter and dance before me my heart knows happiness

this earth, my home
in life and in death

| 5 |

The Wind

The wind arrived in the night howling down the chimney
rocking a door backwards and forwards with an irritating squeak,
squeak
whistling through cracks and under gaps a loud and insistent
intruder

The wind stole my mind and for a moment, an hour, a day, a life-
time
I walked across windswept terrain
a coat strained tight around me
hair blowing, eyes weeping, nose running

I am the howling wind
the bending tree
the rocking door
the choppy sea . . . .
the windswept landscape envelops me

| 6 |

Dark Moon

There is no blood time yet I circle and cycle still
At the dark moon
I taste possibility
I see the beauty and strength of the shadow

The howling wolf
the ravenous raven
the coiled serpent
I let them dance within me feel their magic
the serpent uncoiling
to the beat of the drum and the echo of the call
the call of the wild

Roar, run, screech, soar, hiss, hum, flee, run
skip, dance, sing, scream
Dark magic potent dream

| 7 |

The Shaman

The shaman spat a stream of seeds and soil from her mouth "Grow harmoniously" she said, with tenderness, "grow into an oasis of love".

She bent softly and touched the soil at her feet.

She stood and slowly stepped the circumference of a circle.
As she circled she chanted
      Air moves us
      Fire transforms us
      Water shapes us
      Earth heals us
And the balance of the wheel goes round and round
The balance of the wheel goes round.

Can you dig a culture of strong women?

Life

| 8 |

Death of A Brother

Why did you die
Right there
Right then

A white woman's tears stream down her face

You have become the native of her nightmares
As she sees your lifeless temple
And tastes the futility of trying to save you

Again and again

Who are you?

What is your dreaming?

Have you returned there now?

Was your death as you imagined it?

Why did you die

Right there

Right then

| 9 |

Eleven Percent

Her continuous voice cracks my cranky

silently screaming "Shut the fuck up"
smiling all the while

imagining ice picks, eyes.

Isolation is not responsible

my ears have always been sensitive

and my bullshit radar infallible

She's one of my 11 percent.

| 10 |

Bah Humbug

Christmas cheer pumps out of mechanical Santa's and Snowmen
like the lies from politicians mouths.
Boring, monotonous, painful for the ears and psyche.

Peace on earth, goodwill to all men, unless they perceive you as other.
And none wished to women and especially not those seeking refuge
from violence and oppression.
Another year rolls to an end.
I celebrate the earth's survival and the indomitable human spirit
that continues to cry for justice.

Love and Lust

| 11 |

The Growing Need

She felt it growing. . .
the aching need for physical contact
she could picture the hand stroking her hair
touching her face
exploring it's contours
soft and gentle
yet
awakening the sleeping snake
curled at the base of her spine

She could feel the breath warm on her neck
whispering in her ear
stirring her from the sensual slumber
she'd been in for months

She felt lips
kissing the sides of her face
her neck

nibbling her ear
And all the while the snake was uncurling
rippling slowly through her body
igniting sparks long dormant
building the yearning within her

Could she find that elusive other
who could take her to the precipice of passion
and see her soar

the other who would learn her body's
rhythms and moods and know when gentle touch was needed
and when hard, wild loving was what she craved
She felt it growing . . . the aching need
to be touched by another.

| 12 |

You

Your poetic intelligence ignites my desire,
I want to lick your brain
and feel your words course over me
caressing me like silk

Your energy circles and I,
lost in sleep breathe you in
waking in the morning
knowing the depth of your absence

| 13 |

Sensuous Sunshine

Sunshine seeps through the window softly caressing visible skin
sensuously creeping underneath garments
Slowing an awakening
that this sensuous warmth has arrived
at your sex

Juiciness flows into belly, legs, chest, breast, mind
succulent images arise
The hummingbird sipping nectar
the bee pollinating a rose
a tree bending with the breeze

Desire steals breath

| 14 |

Haiku Song

To my one I sing
Haiku pattern weaving lace
Our love is pure grace

We dance colourful
Inviting arms seek passions
Taste on ruby lips

Green eyes mesmerise
Drawing open abundance
Love flowing freely

Bodies liquefy
Every sense fired alight
Lets melt together

| 15 |

Monsoon Moist

Monsoon season and its wet, moist.
moist are the days
moist are the nights

Moist are my thighs when I think of you
and how I want your tongue telling me
what I can do to please you.

Moist are my thighs when I think of you
and how I want your tongue telling me
how you will please me.

Moist are my thighs when I imagine your lips
beading with monsoonal moisture
that I want to suck from you.

Moist are my thighs when I imagine my tongue
slow dancing across your contours

sipping, slurping your heat.

Moist are my thighs when I imagine taking you
like a monsoonal storm
lightning, thunder,
and you in your nakedness pouring moisture.

| 16 |

Green Finger

Are you jealous of the finger that touches her face
Are you jealous of the finger that down her neck does trace
Are you jealous of the finger pushing back her hair
Are you jealous of the finger going everywhere
Are you jealous of the finger resting on her belly
Are you jealous of the finger turning her legs to jelly
Are you jealous of the finger that now has her moaning
Are you jealous of that finger and wishing it, you were owning?

You've got a green finger!

| 17 |

Nonchalant

How do I stay nonchalant when you take my breath away

How do I stay nonchalant when you invade my thoughts night and day

How do I stay nonchalant waiting for a call

How do I stay nonchalant when I know how hard I fall

under the spell of the possibility of US the possibility of love

the possibility of wanting

the possibility of being wanted

Only in isolation can I remain nonchalant

Unravelling

Invisible chains tied us holding us tight together
at least that's what I thought
until you slipped the bonds
and sent me free falling.

I narrowly escaped despair's abyss
instead a slow unravelling
of the bindings that tie my heart, mind and soul to you.

Soon the cravings will pass and you will be but an echo
in the chambers of my heart.

Politics and Power

| 19 |

Ode to the Last Story

She called it the last story and in it she dreamed how we would all come together peacefully and have a huge pow wow
and we'd tell stories and celebrate the struggles we went through to save the earth from its warring, destructive state.

I used to read that story and feel hope in my heart and believe in a world where we are not torn apart by ridiculous divisions based on colour and creed and unnecessary destruction just for the sake of greed.

I would dream a world of peace where common sense prevailed
and there would be love and support for anyone who ailed and the earth would provide enough for us all to share and in return, for the earth we would care.

My blinkers have come off now
And I'm feeling quiet despair
Because I keep encountering people
Who simply do not care

For our mother earth
And some of her people.

One Sunday I heard how little was being done
in the Northern territory to harness the energy of the sun
And I didn't know there was a cost for not reaching an agreed benchmark.
Did you all know of the many million dollar fine or were you too in the dark?

Then on the Monday I was having dinner with some friends
And I found my tolerance truly has an end
For someone (not my friend) suggested that the Arabs have to go
And nuclear weapons would provide an awesome show
And rid the world of the middle east
Right then my tolerance ceased.

I told that man how disgusting I thought his idea was and left
I felt bereft
The notion that one person could advocate
Such wholesale genocide
It feels too late
to stop the tide
of hatred that's been washing
 over our country and the world
I want the dream back
The dream that unfurled
when I read the Last Story.

| 20 |

Abbott Stew

Abbott, rhymes with rabbit
And like that pestilent creature
He shows no regard for the damage caused to the environment
Or ecological balance

Abbott, rhymes with rabbit
In a frenzy breeding
Bigots and fear-mongers, Racists and haters.

Abbott, rhymes with rabbit
And so too does he hide out in burrows
To avoid those who want rid of him.

Abbott, rhymes with rabbit
But I don't think he'd taste good in any stew
Regardless of the amount of red wine added.

| 21 |

Soil-can you dig it?

In Kenya, I was told by my friend Emily when a baby is born the mothers bury the placenta in the soil.

If they want their child to travel,
mothers bury the placenta in the soil by the river.
If they want their child to remain at home, usually the destiny of the eldest, they bury the placenta in the soil close to the village.
That life-affirming ritual nourishes the soil.

Kenya has changed, as have so many other countries. Impacted by climate change and war in their own and neighbouring countries, more people are fleeing from elements they have no control over.

I wonder about those people who have had to flee
whose placentas are buried in their village,

will they ever again walk the soil of their country?
Will they ever till the soil in their village?
Will their bodies be laid in the soil of their home
so they can nourish it in their death?

Too many have to flee

We have a declaration
A Universal Declaration of Human Rights
It stemmed from understanding the stupidity of war and the havoc it wreaks on lives, on individuals, families, countries.
It stemmed from recognition that in six years too many people had been buried beneath the soil of countries far from their homes.

Yet we persist

Soil doesn't argue
Soil doesn't fight
Do we only understand that once we have returned to soil?

| 22 |

Drone

Once

Harmonic monophonic

Sustained notes

Nourishing soul

Now unmanned military

murderous plane

Destroying body, mind, soul

| 23 |

Suffer not the little children

Sometimes I shed tears for the children in detention centres
the children in refugee camps
the children whose lives are being torn apart by war

Suffer not the little children.

Why then a world plagued by war
our children are worth so much more
than the horror they live in everyday
which is constantly reinforcing to them there is no other way

Violence normalised
populations desensitised
children traumatised
life on earth cannabalised

| 24 |

Rise of the Angry Woman

Androcracy is on the rise again
The world is hostage to the violence of men
Waging wars in homes and battlefields
Who yields? Who yields?

Children lie in terror in their Beds
on their TV's they see fathers losing heads
rape of mothers, daughters, sisters not shown
all alone, all alone

I'm angry
That's for bloody sure
40 years ago I said **Violence no more**
Gylany was cresting on a wave
The beasts had been sent back to their caves

Once again they're out there prowling
And they're howling with open jaws

Revelling in the stench and the horror of their wars
Infanticide, matricide, murder and more
But they go
That's alright fellas, after all we are at war

Gylany knows the depth of grief a parent feels
And gylany knows that love heals
And gylany knows the earth gives us all we need
And all this terror is about being right
Or greed
Domination & control
Who gives a damn about soul and love and art

Yet people be creative when they're being torn apart
By arguments that make no sense
Because they're all about building a fence

That's androcracy
It's not gylany's way
As is making excuses and finding another delay

So the Gylanic people's of the planet earth request
The right to have our values heard
and reflected in the behaviour of our political leaders
And we say stop!
Stop this senseless warring and do it today!

| 25 |

Transmuting Poison

Shhhhhhh
Shhhhhhhh
Listen
Listen do you hear
the sound of fear
the rapidly beating heart
as lives get torn apart

WAR!
what did Frankie goes to Hollywood sing war, what is it good for
absolutely nothing and no-one
except those whose greed for death upon which they feed
appears to never be sated they're always finding
someone new to be hated a new peril
a new terror
a new enemy
oh the havoc we are wreaking
and while some of us are speaking out

this stupid warring is getting to me.

It's sad
It's bad
It's really fucking mad

There is no doubt there is too much destruction
And I want to suction up every ounce of poison
that exists here on this earth
the place of our birth
and I want to transform it transmute it
and spit out something so beautiful
our hearts lift
our fear subsides
we are all welcome no-one hides
doors are open step inside or outside
sit by the fire let's get a little higher
as we sing and hummmmmmmmmmmmmmmmm

www.ingramcontent.com/pod-product-compliance
Lightning Source LLC
Chambersburg PA
CBHW030530010526
44110CB00048B/1061